THE BEST
NEW BRITISH
AND IRISH
POETS
2018

JUDGED AND EDITED BY
MAGGIE SMITH
SERIES EDITOR
TODD SWIFT

THE BEST
NEW BRITISH
AND IRISH
POETS
2018

EYEWEAR PUBLISHING

First published in 2018
by Eyewear Publishing Ltd
Suite 333, 19-21 Crawford Street
Marylebone, London W1H 1PJ
United Kingdom

Cover design and typeset by Edwin Smet
Printed in England by TJ International Ltd, Padstow, Cornwall

ISBN 978-1-912477-04-3

WWW.EYEWEARPUBLISHING.COM

Dedicated to
Menno Wigman (1966-2018)

TABLE OF CONTENTS

INTRODUCTION BY MAGGIE SMITH

On social media, in newspapers and literary journals, and even in casual conversations over a pint, there seems to be a lot of talk about the role of poetry in these strange times – what we expect of it, and what it can and cannot do for us. I've read about poets who will save the world, poems that can heal us, and poetry that saves lives. But I have to wonder: why do we ask a poem to do a job beyond being itself? Why not instead think about what poetry asks – requires – of us? Patience. Attention. Openness. In giving our patience and attention to the poem, and in staying open to the experience of it, we receive the gift of that experience.

When I began selecting poems for this anthology, my approach was simple: to find the best poems. Of course, 'best' is subjective, as is any notion of excellence. I was not seeking poems I expected to heal me or save me, but poems that might shift the furniture in my brain so that it will never go back into those old grooves in the rug again. Poems that may act as lenses long after I read them, allowing me to see anew through them, like the clouds of winter breath in Jack Warren's 'Still Life with Plastic Carrier Bag': 'I used to see my breath in winter air as proof of an inner life – diaphragm/ lungs, sutured into a body that turned/ corners; smiled at strangers in shopping centres.'

Of poetry Keats wrote, 'it should strike the Reader as a wording of his own highest thoughts, and appear almost a Remembrance.' I hope that in these pages, you will discover poems in which you may see yourself, your experiences, and your thinking reflected. I hope you – yes, you! – will find poems to carry with you, poems that give you something you didn't have before opening this book: heightened awareness, an articulation of a feeling, a discovery.

You may wonder if these poems have much in common, other than being written by emerging British and Irish poets. I think as you read through them, you'll see, as I did, a handful of shared thematic concerns: history, family, memory, and landscape. Grief and loss, too, permeate many of the poems you'll encounter here, such as Patrick Wright's 'The End' and Breda Spaight's 'My Mother's Will', but these aren't garden-variety elegies. In Alycia Pirmohamed's 'Elegy on Loop', loss is '[t]his dark grey bar rising like an ugly statistic./ This wild bitterness, unripe blackberry, mouthful/ of dirt.' Sarah Wallis, in 'The World Stands Still to Weep', writes: 'Zero point zero zero two five grams/ is the weight of a tear. Think of the person/ whose job it is to know it,/ to pursue that knowledge in a white coat/ not given to just anyone.' In Hannah Copley's 'Ten Thousand', the grief-stricken is likened to coal, which hardens in darkness: 'Now you sit, heavy and black,/ and wait to make diamonds.' As David McCarthy writes in 'A Denser Dark', '...only the word for flesh/ will be found there, a figure, replacing/ the metaphor for digging, filling the hole/ in the sound we have kept for them.' In poem after poem, from M. J. Arlett's 'Wake' to A. D. Harper's 'Repertory', surprising metaphors reframe and transform universal experiences. What a profound gift for the reader.

You may, like me, be struck by how many poems deal with memory, nostalgia, and coming of age: Alice Kinsella's 'Boy', Shirley Gorby's 'Visiting the Seamstress', and Paul McMahon's 'The Pups in the Boghole.' Some grapple with family history, and memories of parents in particular – Julie Irigaray's 'Tales of the Woodcock',

9

Evan Costigan's 'Winter Picnic', Colin Hassard's 'Flowers', James Finnegan's 'Flood', and Jonathan Totman's 'Explosives Licence' – albeit in fresh and varied ways. Place is essential in poems such as Susan Watson's 'Paul and Clara Walk Beside the Trent', with its lush descriptions of the landscape, and Mariah Whelan's 'Hefted': 'I know here is where my father was happiest – // if I sit on this rock and let the same cold/ enter my body can I say I'm part of it?'

You may notice that a number of the poems deal with the human body, such as O Mayeux, who writes in 'Vessel', 'I became acquainted/ with the strange vehicle of my body.' This 'strange vehicle' is also front and centre in Rosamund Taylor's 'Death's-Head Hawkmoth' ('It's frightening to be so ill./ I take the heat of my body outside…') and Eamon McGuinness's terrific 'That's My Body':

> That's my body, the one you're still carrying,
> bulging, with the tag still on, documents lost,
> nails grown back, tongue freshly painted,
> my body, holding generations, forgotten.

Audrey Molloy's 'Symphony of Skin' skillfully extends the metaphor from the body ('timpani buttoned under a cashier's blouse') to lovers and 'the music of skin.' In poems such as Reiss McGuinness's 'The Silent Treatment' and Nicola Daly's 'Skin Boutique', we see how far apart and how close two people can be, physically and emotionally.

I have to admit, as an American poet, I wondered if I might notice distinct differences in tone or technique in these poems. If anything, I found quite the opposite. Craft elements such as enjambment, anaphora, juxtaposition, and relaxed diction are as prevalent in these poems as they are in so many of my favourites written by American poets. There's a thrilling sense of play throughout this anthology; the poets experiment and take risks, often stitching together seemingly disparate concepts. Cian Murphy's 'At the Clinic' connects landscape and the body, exploring the metaphor of excavation through what is happening outside ('A yellow digger reaches underneath/ to shift earth from the bedrock) and inside ('the x-ray extends/ on its accordion arm and thunks as// it finds its target'). Fiona Cartwright's 'Whalelight' explores two parallel dissections performed by the same man. On the left margin, sixteenth-century French naturalist Guillaume Rondelet dissects a whale, and on the right, he performs his own infant son's autopsy.

> Deeper into the chest he goes, to find
> huge and songless copies
> of the lungs
>
> >   from his own son's chest,
> >   bronchioles branching like winter trees.

Other poems bring in multiple perspectives or even multiple voices, such as Anne Cousins' 'Brooch', Shauna Robertson's 'Ginger', Mary Jean Chan's '//', and James White's 'Astrobiology.' In White's poem, the dialogue is sewn seamlessly into the poem:

> Question for the warden
> after the fifth class: did you know
> koi fish have teeth? Prisoner X told me
> they're in the back of their throat.
>
> It's just, what a place to keep the important things.

11

In Chan's poem, the words of the speaker's mother are both paraphrased and translated in brackets

> To the Chinese,
>
> > you and I are chopsticks: lovers with the same anatomies.
> > My mother tells you that chopsticks in Cantonese sounds
> >
> > like the swift arrival of sons. My mother-tongue rejoices
> > in its dumbness before you as expletives detonate: [two
> >
> > women] [two men] [disgrace].

I admire how Chan's couplets formally enact the couples in the poem – the speaker and her lover, the daughter and her mother. The long lines even look like pair after pair of chopsticks.

There is plenty of formal invention in these pages, notably Fiona Larkin's pantoum, 'Narcissus Consults Google Maps', which cleverly merges myth and modern technology; Michael Ray's use of the imperative to instruct the reader in 'Zest'; Dominic Hand's confident use of white space and jagged lines in 'Night Crossing'; and Emily Holt's 'Interfaced', which eschews conventional syntax and punctuation for a more fragmented, jarring experience. Michael Dooley's 'Anathema', Cynthia Miller's 'Aubade with Court Ruling', and Carina Hart's 'Change Management with Noah' all employ anaphora, as does Kerry Priest's 'The unintentional side-benefits of a slow and premature death', with its brilliant use of gallows humour. The poems are dense with music, from assonance in Joe Carrick-Varty's 'Your Bicycle' ('ducking the rosebush/ to find nothing but the jungle') to a layering of sound play in Sarah Stutt's 'Letatlin' ('thick, simple fingers', 'silk-skinned wings', 'hearts are darkening'),

Caroline Hardaker's 'A hermit crab makes his home inside a doll's head', Christian Wethered's 'Lethe', and Alexandra Strnad's 'The Eyemouth Tapestry':

> …Their hair turns the colour
> of October, tides peel a bride's
> cheek to bone, sands sink her feet.

Kate Arthur's 'Tree' masterfully employs internal rhyme (sound/ground, flight/light, follow/elbow), and Geraldine Clarkson's 'Inisnee' is full of delightful play and pleasure in language. These are deftly crafted poems that succeed on the page but beg to live in our mouths and in the air.

Despite any thematic or formal commonalities, I think you'll find plenty of diversity in voice and approach in these pages. Each poem speaks for itself. Each poem is 'best'. But if I had to select one word to describe the poems, it might be inventive. I was struck by how each poem is a feat of imagination and intelligence, each poet an inventor. They have made whole worlds from scratch, fleshing them out with gorgeous detail, and they have invited us inside. Joe Caldwell's 'Bright Idea' asks the reader to consider life '[b]efore the sun was invented.' Shannon Kelly's 'Bucharest, 1989', imagines life '[w]hen all of this is over.' Kelly's images are deliciously specific and compelling:

> There will be a group of bony men
> in all black who stumble around,
> slipping into foundational cracks,
> helping themselves to the furs inside,
> picking red flecks off the swimming pool mosaic.

Caroline Boreham's 'Helicopter' begins:

13

On the news a copter flew over a tribe
that hasn't been filmed yet
and they were standing and watching under
oversized clumps of leaf.

This poem not only engages the imagination but also speaks to a wider world and larger concerns.

Curating this collection of fifty excellent poems has been such a treat for me, and it heartens me to know that these poets will find new readers for their work via this book, and that you, dear reader, may find some new favourite poets. If you approach these poems with openness, if you give them your full attention, and if you are patient, you will close this book with something you didn't have when you opened it – perhaps a new take on the new year, which 'comes/....like a barrel over a waterfall/ like me, inside a barrel, over a waterfall' (Lenni Sanders' 'NYE'). If nothing else, I hope you will be convinced of the talented new poets in your midst, and of the vitality of contemporary British and Irish poetry.

M. J. ARLETT
was born in the UK,
grew up in Spain, and now lives in
Texas where she is pursuing her PhD.
She is a founding editor at the
Plath Poetry Project.

WAKE

The five senses are a lie I don't remember
being told. No mention of pressure, pain,

or how we know something is wrong,
a sullen lingering on the hillside.

The boxes are packed, boarding passes printed,
and our mother is waiting to pick us up in England.

In the half-occupied master bedroom, an incessant
robot is chirping. Distant. Not enough to disturb

my sister who sleeps wearing a tiara,
clutching an over-loved polar bear. Not even

enough to wake me, at first. Only when the abrasive
notes cut into the crevasse of my sleep

do I rouse, confused, and pad the hallway to the far
side of the house. I've come to learn

the body can enact what the mind wants
without permission, how maybe my father

more than anything wanted to keep his family whole,
the only way to do so

to sleep through the day
of our leaving. His big toe emerging from the white plains

of the bed, the grating alarm beside his head,
and little me, poised at the foot,

trying to determine if his chest was a watch
in need of winding.

— first appeared in *RHINO*

KATE CAOIMHE ARTHUR

was born in Northern Ireland
in 1979, and now lives in Cambridgeshire.
She became Fenland Poet Laureate
in March 2017.

TREE

Running is never enough
I am listening for the sound
of the ground saying Here
or perhaps a bird flight
arching above it or light pool
from a shaft of sun
Home. Where can I plant us.
Follow the lockspit
to the elbow of the fen
Looking for a clearing
or a piece of scrub
where I can dig a hole,
a burrow, damp with dew
An oak tree, wrecked by wind
I found it, and a red fox
white tailed
Why must I be an animal
to hide in this place

In our bed, these nights
I dig into you with
Fingers, tongue, nails.

– first appeared in *The Fenland Reed*

CAROLINE BOREHAM
was born in Manchester,
grew up in the Peak District and
now lives in York. She has been shortlisted
five times for the Bridport
Poetry Prize.

HELICOPTER

On the news a copter flew over a tribe
that hasn't been filmed yet
and they were standing and watching under
oversized clumps of leaf.
It said they were the last free people in the world
and that protecting them didn't mean just
leaving them alone. It said they were important
because they showed a different way of life was possible.
When I think of that place, I think of the trees
as extensive but
my life as small, that is to say
it was not the only thing there was, there was space in it
for new people and things, space outside it
in which to be free. A complete history
in the soil, enough of it
to soak everything up like a sponge.
Now I live in a floodplain, there is no getting a view
and although the flood's expansive
when you can see the sky in it, it's what's left over
that isn't. They have to hose down the walkways
before anyone can walk on them. It's expensive, shows
we only just manage to get away with this.
I'm not saying I don't like my creature comforts.
I don't think there is anyone important left to meet.
I don't think there is enough of it
to soak everything up like a sponge
or that trees can be big enough lungs, the sea
a big enough liver.
I want the same for my daughter as everyone else.
It's all competing claims now.
I know there are different sorts of freedom, like freedom from
fluctuation in resources.

The trees here rot
from the soaking their roots keep getting and if
there's a question about the safety of one of them
it has to go anyway and my life is big, insofar as
it's at its max and shrill in my ears.
When I first fell for him
he was the sky the sea, but even that turned out to be an illusion of
sustainability.
And if there is a place like that anymore
the trees are in undersized clumps
that are of no use to anyone anymore
because they are not part of what is known
as a green corridor.

JOE CALDWELL

was born in Sheffield in 1982.
As well as writing, he teaches English
in a secondary school. His poems have been
published in *The Rialto*, *The North*, *Under the
Radar*, and various other magazines
and anthologies.

BRIGHT IDEA

Before the sun was invented,
we'd to keep the streetlights burning
all day, and the sky always felt

empty, though we knew God was there,
and we still enjoyed those mornings
it was a cold confident blue.

Most history books say Britain
was the first country to come up
with sun, though you do hear nowadays

it was brought back from America.
People talk about the end of
rationing, but when the sun

was invented, that *was* a change.
Just walking about, you felt happy.
It was like a new haircut, or love.

People gazed at it, it stopped traffic,
it filled up the surgeries with folk
who didn't realise that you mustn't stare.

– first appeared in *Butcher's Dog*

JOE CARRICK-VARTY

was born in Oxford in 1993
and read English Literature with Creative
Writing at the University of Manchester. His
work has appeared in *The Interpreter's House*,
And Other Poems and *Brittle Star* amongst other
places. Based in Manchester, Joe is currently
studying for a Master's at The Centre for
New Writing.

YOUR BICYCLE

That morning in 1993, the lawn misting,
unkept at the wall where we'd dug the hole
for the pond that we abandoned,
your bicycle, with spokes and chain

grown through, tangled, leant by itself.
The shape it left lasted a second;
first the wheels, then the pedals
stiff and locked, rusted, stuck to the honeysuckle

curled on the frame. Might the garden be in on this?
Might you, one day, come home, step out
over the gravel, ducking the rosebush
to find nothing but the jungle I haven't weeded since?

Or might you know already
about the snail I found there, about the webs
hung between the rubber handle and the wall,
the bell full up with lichen, moss, earwigs,

those woodlice in the brake pedals?
The grass tugged a little, and let go with a slow rip.
Uprooted, then coiling back
into place like a fist so intent on keeping hold.

– first appeared in *Crannóg Magazine*

FIONA CARTWRIGHT

was born in London and lives
in Surrey. She has a PhD in animal ecology
and works as a post-doctoral conservation
scientist. Her poems have appeared in various
publications, including *Mslexia*, *Butcher's Dog*,
Envoi and *Ink, Sweat & Tears*.

WHALELIGHT

Rondelet dangles one ribcage from the ceiling
like a chandelier,
each rib a crescent moon
reflecting its own light
from the whale oil plumping up his lamp.
He selects his largest scalpel, cuts
the animal
blubbering on his table, making
a hole in the unscaled skin
that calls to mind

                    his son's creaturely pelt, that initial give
               on incision, then the resistance of the body
                    that has swum from salt water
                           still wearing fur
                which should have been dropped
                    like a coat to the floor

as the whale dropped hers. Rondelet
stretches one flipper
and holds her metacarpals with his own –

                       his own son's fingers.
                He could close the whale's hand
                  over a million infant digits
               but the structure is unchanged.

Deeper into the chest he goes, to find
huge and songless copies
of the lungs

                          from his own son's chest,
            bronchioles branching like winter trees.

Beneath the ribs
there is a womb –

his wife's pregnant belly
whalebacking from the bath,
his son inside,
drinking salt water in the dark
like a whale's mooncalf
never seeing
by the light of a whale.

— first appeared in *Envoi*

Guillaume Rondelet was a 16th century French naturalist who dissected whales, concluding that they were mammals, not fish. He also performed an autopsy on his infant son to establish cause of death.

MARY JEAN CHAN

is a poet and editor from Hong Kong.
A graduate of Swarthmore College, the University of Oxford and Royal Holloway, she is a PhD candidate in Creative Writing, Research Associate in Poetics and Visiting Lecturer at Royal Holloway. Her debut pamphlet, *A Hurry of English*, is published by ignitionpress. Mary Jean has been shortlisted for the 2017 Forward Prize for Best Single Poem, the 2016 London Magazine Poetry Prize and the 2016 Resurgence Poetry Prize (Commended), and is the winner of the 2017 PSA/Journal of Postcolonial Writing Postgraduate Essay Prize, the 2017 Psychoanalysis and Poetry Competition, the 2017 Poetry Society Members' Competition and the 2016 Oxford Brookes International Poetry Competition (ESL). Mary Jean is a Ledbury Emerging Poetry Critic and a Co-Editor at *Oxford Poetry*.

//

My mother lays the table with chopsticks & ceramic
spoons, expects you to fail at dinner. To the Chinese,

you and I are chopsticks: lovers with the same anatomies.
My mother tells you that *chopsticks* in Cantonese sounds

like *the swift arrival of sons*. My mother tongue rejoices
in its dumbness before you as expletives detonate: *[two*

women] [two men] [disgrace]. Tonight, I forget that I am
bilingual. I lose my voice in your mouth, kiss till blood

comes so *sorry* does not slip on an avalanche of syllables
into sorrow. I tell you that as long as we hold each other,

no apology will be enough. Tonight, I am dreaming again
of tomorrow: another chance to eat at the feast of the living

with chopsticks balanced across the bridges of our hands
as we imbibe each *yes*, spit out every *no* among scraps of

shell or bone. Father says: *kids these days are not as tough*
as we used to be. So many suicides in one week. How many

times have you and I wondered about leaving our bodies
behind, the way many of us have already left? My friend's

sister loved a woman for ten years and each word she says
to her mother stings like a papercut. Each word she does

not say burns like the lines she etches carefully into skin.
I have stopped believing that secrets are a beautiful way

to die. You came home with me for three hundred days —
to show my family that dinner together won't kill us all.

31

— first appeared in *Ambit Magazine*

GERALDINE CLARKSON

was born in Warwickshire, UK, with roots in the west of Ireland. Her poems have appeared in *Poetry Magazine, The Poetry Review, Poetry London, Ambit,* and *The Rialto,* and have been broadcast from the Royal Albert Hall as part of the BBC Radio 3 Proms Extra series. She has two pamphlets: *Declare* (Shearsman Books, 2016), which was selected as a Poetry Book Society Pamphlet choice, and *Dora Incites the Sea-Scribbler to Lament* (smith|doorstop, 2016), which was a Laureate's Choice. She is a former winner of the *Poetry London* and *Ambit* competitions, as well as the Poetry Society Anne Born and *Magma* Editors' prizes.

INISNEE

Call it Inish-nee, nee, nee, with twelve permutations of Nee in ten
generations, six gorse-humped fields, three starved white beaches
with dozens of deep knock-kneed inlets, and seven headscarved
sisters, living together as seamstresses, unmarried, Conneellys.
Bridgie used to come over from their house by boat for Mass

on the mainland. Now a bridge links the two
and she's stopped practising. Scarlet-sailed hookers cut
the caul of silk water. Weeds stink in the shallows.
No longer making shawls but mending fishing nets and darning
Aran sweaters for tourists, she's started swearing, her mind like a sewer.

– first appeared in *Shearsman Magazine*

HANNAH COPLEY

is an academic and writer.
She completed her PhD at the University
of Leeds, where she researched the poetry and
archives of Geoffrey Hill, Jon Silkin, and Tony
Harrison. She was one of ten highly commend-
ed poets in the 2015/16 Faber New Poets Prize
and in 2017 she was highly commended in the
Hippocrates Prize. Her work has been published
extensively in magazines and anthologies.

TEN THOUSAND

All the ways a person can be made
to understand the darkness in their heart —

to know they've been lost —
can be traced back to coal.

Coal, through and through.
Coal. It's a better rule to live by,

singing as it does of *the earth's inside,*
of stain and cinder, of burning

red like the raw edges of a wound.
Coal. It's what grief becomes

if pressed upon, moment
after moment added to the pile.

Some hurts aren't meant to disappear
but to blacken,

to roll in on themselves and stoke up,
ready for the blaze.

Like that cough you've had
since the day your daughter died.

That is coal. That is the inside too.
The black bile peats, hardens,

ready to hock itself up
in a cloud of smoke and soot.

Ten thousand days
is long enough to line your lungs.

Now you sit, heavy and black,
and wait to make diamonds.

– first appeared in *Verse Matters*

EVAN COSTIGAN

was born in Dublin in 1976.

His poems have been published in *Poetry Ireland Review, The Stinging Fly, The Irish Times, The Moth, The Stony Thursday Book, Cyphers* and elsewhere. Selected for the 2016 Poetry Ireland Introductions Series, he is a past winner of the Boyle Arts Festival Poetry Competition and the Francis Ledwidge International Poetry Award.

In 2017 he won the Red Line Book Festival Poetry Competition and the Oliver Goldsmith Literary Festival Poetry Competition. He was shortlisted for a Hennessy Literary Award in 2014. He has lived abroad most of his adult life, but now divides his time between the west coast of Ireland and Dublin, where he works as a creative writing facilitator.

WINTER PICNIC

Whenever my father returned from his travels, the house filled with tales
of moaning bears and night skies fractured by the branches of trees
he'd rolled his bed under. Jade and camel-bone snuff bottles
bullied rock fragments to the precipice of our mantelpiece.

There were mornings we woke to new alphabets on bedroom walls
or the bugled blast of a *sankha* last sounded on monastery grounds,
where he'd persuaded a monk to barter it for a penknife. He spoke
of the ruby-red eye of a hare in the Arctic, sudden blizzards,

spheres of perfect silence, a beast abominable only
in its loneliness. Within weeks, he grew quiet, until the tug
of the next adventure. We were bolder in his absence.
That day we emerged from the brambly tundra of the lower garden,

arms and faces scissored by briars, to burst into the attic. I flung open
the battered suitcase with broken clasps. Inside were letters
tied with twine, Sellotaped maps, out-of-shape matchboxes
that rattled with the husks of winged insects. We found a journal.

Opened, it released a withered stem for a bookmark. There were faint
sketches of flowers, a bird with a Mohawk of feathers. On a loose page,
the portrait of a woman with a hook nose, her eyes pencil-grey tones.
An entry: *Fatherhood?*

That last trip. His face shaggy as a yak when he got back; how he
hugged each one of us and then hung on. An excursion our mother
forbade we ask about; from our listening post on the stairs, we learned of
a dust storm so fierce he thought the world was coming undone.

After he remained, we had lessons in languages, our dreams swelled
with seas of moving grasses, snake charmers, the call to prayer.
Most of all, I remember that picnic. The five of us on a blanket,
drinking tea from small glasses under trees stripped of leaves.

38

– first appeared in *Poetry Ireland Review*

ANNE COUSINS

began to write poetry
after completing her MA in Creative
Writing (University College Dublin, 2013).
Her work has appeared in various literary
magazines including *Poetry Ireland Review; The
Best New British and Irish Poets 2017; The Stinging
Fly, The SHOp, The Honest Ulsterman,* and was
Highly Commended in The Patrick Kavanagh
Poetry Competition 2015 and in 2016. She was
born in 1958 in County Wexford, Ireland and
still lives there.

BROOCH

for Jean McConville (1934-1972)

Trussed up like an old hen – and sulking
when we pulled the sack off. A touch
of steel under her ear persuaded her.

I'd say it was a fair trial – rigorous maybe –
but we gave her time and more than one chance
to tell the truth and shame the devil.

She said it began with a knock, a thump
like a bag of coal falling and there he was –
a wee fellow – dying on her threshold.

We heard she had provided a cushion.
'A pillow,' she said, 'that's all it was.'
I recall the crack of my boot to her head.

The Chief was kind, patient as a saint.
'Tell us all,' he coaxed, 'and you'll be back
with the weans by Bingo time.'

I held a cigarette to her mouth, pulled
off her wedding-ring. We left her in her cardi,
an old nappy-pin on the lapel.

It's that pin that haunts my sleep –
warrior-mother's rust-bronzed brooch,
sole relic of the Disappeared.

NICOLA DALY

has had poetry and prose published in maga-
zines such as *The North, The Rialto, Mslexia* and
many more. Her short stories have appeared in
publications such as Honno anthologies and *The
Stinging Fly*. In 2017 she came third in the Welsh
Writing Awards organised by the *New Welsh
Review*.

THE SKIN BOUTIQUE

All as I ever wanted was sweetbreads and sticky figs
but my lover gifted me a silk purse made from a sow's ear.

I wanted the complete works of Shakespeare
but he gave me a necklace of pig's teeth and earrings made from tusk.

I hinted at a pair of shoes with pointed toes, in the palest blue
yet he garbed me in mink and Moroccan kid
and went on to barter for my soul with the blunt discarded bones of beasts.

I never asked for this reek of sanguine mingled with lust
nor the weekly drive to the skin boutique.

Yet he feeds me on sweetbreads and sticky figs.
He gives me my shoes, silk purse and the softest gloves.

So I allow him to cover my sex in the tang of leather,
my spine in fur and my breasts in feathers.

MICHAEL DOOLEY

was born in Limerick in 1986. His poetry has
been published in literary journals in Ireland, the
UK, and the USA. In 2016, he was shortlisted for
the Dermot Healy International Poetry Com-
petition and highly commended in the Patrick
Kavanagh Poetry Award. In 2017, he was joint
runner-up in the inaugural Mairtín Crawford
Award. He studied at The National University
of Ireland, Galway, and is a teacher.

ANATHEMA

He broke horses when chasers
Were in the paddock on slow wet afternoons –
Broke the careful silence of a newly backed filly:
'Treat the reins as if they were velvet'.

He broke fasts with dawn prayers
Under cracked-ridge saddles
And paint-flakes held in cobweb –
Murmurs of Leviticus.

He broke his nose in an alley
In Charleville in nineteen eighty-two
Fighting a traveller
For five hundred pounds.

He broke himself
In fits of compunction, sending
What little he had to Africa,
Or to a satellite Evangelical.

He broke the yellow
Stained glass of the
Back-door when he
Was 'put through it'.

He broke his skin,
Leaning over
A shotgun,
In nineteen ninety-four.

He broke his wife.

Horses, in exhaustion,
Horses.

– first appeared in *The Stinging Fly*

JAMES FINNEGAN

In 2016, Dublin-born Finnegan
was highly commended in the Patrick
Kavanagh Poetry Award, shortlisted for Over
The Edge New Writer of the Year, published in
The Bombay Review and *The Canterbury Festival
Anthology for Poet of the Year 2016*. In 2017 he was
published in *Skylight47*, *Sarasvati*, *North West
Words* and *CYPHERS*, and had three poems
printed in the *Canterbury Festival Anthology for
Poet of The Year 2017*. Two of Finnegan's poems
featured in New Irish Writing in *The Irish Times*.
Finnegan taught in St Eunan's College, Letterk-
enny, holds a doctor of philosophy in living ed-
ucational theory and has a first full collection of
poems forthcoming in June 2018 with Eyewear
Publishing.

FLOOD

my father and I stride to early Mass
downhill from Castletown Cross
past Matthews' old house   its hedge
once hid our sibling gang for half a day
     before our brother Francis left us

past horses   past wired canvas tents   past clotheslines
past rusted pots with steaming water
all the way to the flooded road
which blocks our short-cut to St Joseph's
I then hear my father say *fuck*

and in an instant
there is a lesser saint
in the man who leads me through water

– first appeared in *SKYLIGHT 47*

SHIRLEY GORBY

lives in Dublin. In 2017,
her work featured in *The Irish Times*
as part of the Hennessey New Irish
Writing and also in *Poetry
Ireland Review*.

VISITING THE SEAMSTRESS

The bulb's flash calls her to the door.
She cannot hear or speak, but smiles
leading mother and I down the hall
to a room that smells of cloth
sewn with threads of smoke,
where the sewing machine faces a wall.

On a table by the window, a cup of biros,
a stack of paper – unlined square sheets
like baking parchment, yet lighter.
Their writing hands –
mouths with voices of ink;
gossip flows onto empty sheets.

In laughter the shrill sound
of my mother intrudes,
and so I choose
not to hear, but watch
two faces, two bodies uncontrollably move
toward each other and back.

I read used pages
and crumpling the names of neighbours
and mothers of school friends
into the bad happenings penned,
my hands become feet
trampling leaves to a whisper.

On leaving the silence of that house,
a wastepaper basket brims
with an afternoon's conversation,
bar one sheet of paper that lies

hidden in a child's coat pocket;
so deftly folded onto itself,
it can no longer breathe.

– first appeared in *Poetry Ireland Review*

DOMINIC HAND

is a young Irish poet based
in Oxford (b.1995). He studied English
Literature at Oriel College, Oxford University, and wrote his thesis on the poetry of J. H.
Prynne. He won Oxford University's Newdigate Prize in 2017, the Christopher Tower Poetry Prize in 2014 and was named a Foyle Young
Poet in 2013. His work has been published in
numerous journals in the UK and US, including
Oxford Poetry, *The Missing Slate*, *Poetry*, *Process*,
The Mays, *Playhouse64* and *Isis Magazine*.

NIGHT CROSSING

Bound to a rafter, mouth cupped
       in silence at the keel, the pitch-black water
             flickers like diesel oil
trailing the ligature of the sea's tract caught
between two states
of movement. Here, one might sprint
       out of the hot shade
down the shoreline's lip, to glance across the other,
       opposite bank. Inland,
the pines are angled by the zither of the wind, the gulf's heat
           rising into bars
       that hang above the water. Here, to believe such a journey
           is possible – that one might spread outwards
through this multitude of sand
and white skin – is to beg
to live.

      ★

A sirocco grinds against the dust-
           green boughs of the olive trees,
the thinning shrublands.
Sunless,
people have traversed this path together –
       walking through walls
of ocean air, the blurred vibrations of the landscape
           under haphazard candlelight.
They have watched the darkness striating
into less.
Across the mercurial water,
the washed-up eyes
       of stones are spat up

through the porous scrag of coral,
branching off

          in speared tongues.

Now, a salt-cracked gorge
splits the boat's hyphen
from its severed point
    of contact
to break open like a tear duct,
arriving in one final stroke –
lungs tensing
like a pitched tent.

       ★

How do we answer this call? –
this broken voice? – the one
      we press into silence, turn
            away at the door?

This sound that comes
      from nowhere – a glass harmonica
    at sea –
           is it authorised?
    Is it legal?

And when it fades, will you look back
      at them in the eyes? even
          notice their colours?

I will keep my face low to the ground, one says,

I will tune my voice to yours.

CAROLINE HARDAKER

lives in Newcastle upon Tyne. Her
poetry has been published widely, most
recently by *Magma*, The Emma Press, *Neon*,
and *Shoreline of Infinity*. She is a guest editor for
Three Drops Press, and the in-house blogger
for Mud Press. Her debut chapbook *Bone
Ovation* was published by Valley Press
in October 2017.

A HERMIT CRAB MAKES HIS HOME INSIDE A DOLL'S HEAD

Seated, he is a fist, and when he crawls
an open hand,
his underbelly raw as a fig's middle.
His weakness drags the sand, an immature length
born for burial. Crawl on it,
curl it into the segments of palm.
Pretend it doesn't exist. Seek.
Seek. Slowly seek

and find a sheltering place, a red womb. Here.
A bulbous cove to birth a world in which he's safe,
half within, and half without.
He thrusts a naked thumb inside the head
(up through the neck)
and clamps the cheek behind the teeth
with a cooling uropod, a hook with an eye for darkness.
Such a find, this ruddy pink rock.
Only a limpet or two live within, and on the skin
a pair of sky-cast barnacles watch the stars
for one last time before the deep,
the end, the beginning.

★

Sometimes you see a face in the rock pools.
It scares children, men blink and look away.
A baby's head drags across the sea bed in jolts.
Two white-cast runes, lids always open,
and four legs to crawl with. More eyes on stalks.
Claws.

54

– first appeared in *The Interpreter's House*

A. D. HARPER

was born in London in 1968.
He has worked in science and bookselling.
His poems have appeared in *Rattle*, *The Stinging Fly*, *Butcher's Dog* and *The Interpreter's House*, among others.

REPERTORY

The ambulance end-stops the street and instead of awe
at storybook ritual impressing itself into the domestic
I now hope the nearest relative masters the spiel –
age, medical conditions, timeline of symptoms,
the drugs the patient's taking – the elevator pitch
of facts and spoilers first to the paramedics and then
again in A and E, and then again to the doctor after that,
and then again, until the inner rhythm of the script
reveals itself, the heart of the soliloquy, but then
the staff start talking to each other, details change
or are reordered by professional tradition,
you are the child at prize day, the spotlight passes on,

then darkness, sitting cafeteria-alone bargaining
with God for time unless there's pain then asking
for comfort, or if the diagnosis shifts for long enough
then wanting a clear answer, though you learn the days
still carry on without a name, traffic jams, radio songs,
the car-door slam that isn't them, gameshow applause,
harried experts making guesses, trying interventions,
then ceiling-staring instead of sleep, unable to forget
their caseload, the night too information-rich
so a cosy murder mystery at 2 a.m., a genius, the dead
fictitious, meaningless but always laced with clues,
the relative, discreetly weeping, led offstage in silence.

CARINA HART

was born in Norfolk, UK in 1987.
She is a lecturer in English Literature at the
University of Nottingham Malaysia Campus,
and has been shortlisted for the Overton
Prize and runner up in the Melita
Hume Poetry Prize.

CHANGE MANAGEMENT WITH NOAH

And the Lord said
there must be a top-down rationalisation
by way of fully managed precipitation;
sweep away, root and branch, the old ways.

And the Lord said
processes have been mapped and found inadequate:
the organisation cannot thus move forward.
Below management level all structures must go.

And the Lord said
let it rain for forty days and forty nights
precisely; my executive schedule is tight.
I will wipe from the earth every living creature I have made.

And the Lord said
the redundancies are most regrettable,
but every bird and beast must be accountable
in the final audit.

And the Lord said
we have been much lauded for our transformation.
No there are no plans for reconstruction
until we secure funding for the next phase.

COLIN HASSARD

was born in Belfast in 1982.
He is a two-time Ulster Poetry Slam
Champion, a former NI Human Rights
Festival Writer-in-Residence, and his work
has been performed on BBC Radio. He was
long-listed for the Seamus Heaney Award
for New Writing in 2017 and 2018.

FLOWERS

I hear the scrat of soil being split & lifted –
scattering like clumps of rain,
& follow the sound to my bedroom window.

My mother is kneeling by the flowerbed, planting bulbs.
With hands unhardened in my father's gloves
she rakes the soil knowing what colours will bloom

& when. On a clement April afternoon, she is planning
for summer; painting the garden by numbers; removing
winter as carefully as a surgeon removes cancer.

I watch her like the dove she calls Scruffy
who waits on the bird-house roof each morning
for the ashtray of mixed seed.

Like Scruffy, & the bees, & the insects,
& my father cursing each splutter of the lawnmower,
I can only be a guest in her garden.

She tells my father that her knees are sore,
& he brings her cushion from the garage.
When the lawnmower rumbles, I close the window,

ashamed not to know the names of the flowers.

EMILY HOLT

was born in California in 1988 to Irish parents. She received her MFA from the Rainier Writing Workshop at Pacific Lutheran University and has worked as a teacher, journalist and caregiver in the US, Ireland and Northern Ireland. She currently lives in Dublin. Her essays and poems have appeared in *Brief Encounters: A Collection of Contemporary Nonfiction* (W.W. Norton & Co., 2015), *Poetry Ireland Review*, *The Honest Ulsterman, Abridged* and other journals. She has been a finalist for the 2018 Dermot Healy International Poetry Prize, the 2018 Patrick Kavanagh Poetry Award and the 2016 Dorothea Lange-Paul Taylor Prize at Duke University's Center for Documentary Studies.

INTERFACED

She is always there   the woman
with the plastic mask   on the wall

of the museum   and before that
I'd assume   in the paper the week

the bomb went off   and I wonder
maybe even now   sitting through her own

life   Sanctum   bending
to a granddaughter in a crib   Does she still

wear the mask   I wonder   or was it meant only
for the healing   for the aftermath   the camera?

I wonder   and yet   I find   her face is searchable
the engine numb under my fingers

her life the subject of articles because the issue
of compensation is unresolved and her case –

shrapnel still in her neck and children to feed –
one of the more difficult   you could say

I do say   though now I'm measuring
Lives surely call   for the measuring stick

a wall of distinction   between here and there
a face with scars   and a hand   scarred   a hand striking   and a face

struck by light   too early in the morning

– first appeared in *Talking River*

JULIE IRIGARAY

(b.1993) is a poet from the Basque
Country. Raised in the southwest of France,
she was educated at Trinity College Dublin and
King's College London. Her work has appeared
in various international publications, including
*Ink, Sweat & Tears, Shearsman, Tears in the Fence,
Southword, Banshee, Mslexia, Envoi, The Ofi Press*
and *Every Writer*. She has won third prize in the
2017 Winchester Writers' Festival Poetry Com-
petition and was shortlisted for the 2017 Over
the Edge New Writer of the Year, the Yeovil
Poetry Prize 2017, the 2016 Blackwater Interna-
tional Competition and *The London Magazine*
Poetry Prize 2016.

TALES OF THE WOODCOCK

A picture of me holding a woodcock
my father had freshly shot
takes pride of place in our living room.
What a peculiar thing to let a three-year-old child
pose with a dead bird, and such a majestic one.
But I'm not repelled. I am familiar with

the woodcock's umber and burnt sienna
plumage – I even know her Latin name is
Scolopax rusticola, that her belly resembles
bandages. I have learned to find the pin feathers,
these delicate stripped tears used
by artists as brushes for miniatures.

I spread her wing as one unfolds a moth, trying
not to touch the powder which allows it flight.
I'm not thinking about why her head is dangling:
I just love to caress her coal skullcap. I grasp

the woodcock tightly – my father's most precious
treasure. I don't realise yet that he will neglect
his family to track her down every weekend.
I don't resent her being our rival.

                    *

A snapshot of the mind: I'm no more than twelve
and my mother cooks woodcocks in boiling
duck fat to preserve them. She offers to prepare me
one for breakfast: I accept but feel embarrassed
as I know she is going to tell her friends
and all the family how good a girl from

the southwest I am, eating woodcocks at 9 a.m.:
'Such a strong child, a hunter's daughter.'

Now I feel terribly guilty when I devour the woodcocks
my father shoots. I love the crack of the beak
when I open it to catch the tongue, breaking the skull
to suck the brain, the succulent taste of what I enucleate.
Then I reflect on this pair of obsidian eyes, always glassy
– the most impenetrable I've ever seen. So I make a small
sacrifice by not asking my father to bring me others,
hoping my opposition is of principle, not a rejection of him.

SHANNON KELLY

A native of Lincoln, Nebraska,
Shannon Kelly obtained her BA in English
from the University of St. Thomas in St. Paul,
Minnesota, and recently received her MA in
writing with first-class honours from the National University of Ireland, Galway. Her work
has been featured in *Crannóg*, *The Irish Times*,
BODY Prague, *The Indianapolis Review*, and *Bohemyth*, and she was the 2016 winner of the Allingham Festival Poetry Competition. She currently
resides in Galway, Ireland.

BUCHAREST, 1989

When all of this is over,
there will be an abundance of meat,
milk, and white sugar.

We will find a little television set,
rusted but functional,
tune the antenna,
and watch for hours, if we like.

Every neighbourhood will be our own –
and enough toilet paper to last us
through the next three winters,
the skirmishes on the street.

Our coffee we will drink with relish.
What I do not finish, I will dump
down the drain with no pang of remorse.

When all of this is over,
we will bribe an officer
to let us near that house
where the basement cinema sits empty,
and the bedrooms are broken stale replicas of Versailles.

There will be a group of bony men
in all black who stumble around,
slipping into foundational cracks,
helping themselves to the furs inside,
picking red flecks off the swimming pool mosaic.

Someone will set fire to the front lawn, someone
will savour the last hidden bottle of Maramureş wine,
crawling into a cupboard and sipping it there through wild teeth;
Someone will set the peacocks free.

– first appeared in *Crannóg Magazine*

ALICE KINSELLA

was born in Dublin and raised in Mayo.
She was educated at Trinity College Dublin
and NUI Galway. Her poetry has been widely
published at home and abroad, most recently
in *Banshee Lit, Boyne Berries, The Lonely Crowd,*
and *The Irish Times.* Her work has been listed for
competitions such as Over the Edge New Writer
of the Year Competition 2016, Jonathan Swift
Awards 2016, and Cinnamon Press Pamphlet
Competition 2017. She was SICCDA Liberties
Festival writer in residence for 2017 and received
a John Hewitt bursary in the same year. Her
debut, *Flower Press,* is published with The On-
slaught Press (2018).

BOY

I found you in the garden,
the first day after we had moved in,
stealing apples that had fallen in the wind.
They would only go to the blackbirds
or the earthworms in the dirt,
which would feed the birds anyway.

I showed you the pictures in the sky:
Ursa Major, Pleiades, Cassiopeia.
You told me the proper names:
The Plough, Seven Sisters,
but could not see *Cassiopeia*
no matter how much I pointed.

You taught me that the bite in the apple
had gone to feed something else,
and that the crescent moon
is just a fraction of the whole.

FIONA LARKIN

was born in London in 1965
to Irish parents, read English at St Edmund Hall,
Oxford, and has just completed an MA in Crea-
tive Writing at Royal Holloway. She has worked
for the Bank of England and in the education
sector. Her work appears widely in journals,
including *The North*, *Magma*, *And Other Poems*,
Under the Radar and *Envoi*, and was Commended
in the Café Writers Competition 2017.

NARCISSUS CONSULTS GOOGLE MAPS

The world revolves around me
when I press your little arrow.
I touch an icon on the screen
and I'm spotlit, on location.

When I press your little arrow
I'm the centre of my planet.
Blue-spotlit, on location –
my aura magnetises.

I'm the centre of my planet,
and the satellite agrees.
My aura magnetises
his paparazzo orbit.

The satellite agrees
all road signs lead to me.
His paparazzo orbit
zooms in on starlit filters.

All road signs lead to me,
brightest icon on the screen.
Zoom in on starlit filters:
the world revolves around me.

– first appeared in *The North*

O MAYEUX

was born in London
in 1992 and grew up between
Scotland and Nigeria. He is currently
a PhD candidate in sociolinguistics at the
University of Cambridge, where he researches
Louisiana Creole, his endangered heritage
language. O Mayeux's poetry and
language art has appeared in a
number of publications in
the UK and the US.

VESSEL

So it was that I became acquainted
with the strange vehicle of my body.

For years, the mind had campaigned
ruthlessly for independence and
a strict centralisation of power.

Parts of the body turned red,
bled in protest; the heart
beat itself arrhythmic.

My voice, sweet orphan
of my lungs, hidden
darkly within,

My voice emerged,

Speaking in tongues.

– first appeared in *Assaracus*

DAVID McCARTHY,

a recovering academic, lives in Dublin
and is currently working on his first collection,
Mute Variations, to which this poem belongs. His
work has previously appeared in *A New Ulster*
and *Dodging the Rain*.

A DENSER DARK

after Catherine Corless

Within what is said you keep silence,
possessing nothing, where names are
inscribed, forgotten before they were
spoken, each marking a moment of
atonement, extending toward and
beyond us, who listen for the syllables
from this other side, an otherwise,
never present or contemporary to itself.

Memory needs a more tangible grammar,
a gesture, part of the part that was the
beginning, but only the word for flesh
will be found there, a figure, replacing
the metaphor for digging, filling the hole
in the sound we have kept for them.

A denser dark surrounds us, confirmed
by its contrary, without which no one
disappears, stones echo speech, inert
verbs for now – here, everything else
remains immovable, except this mass of
nothing, remembering what we forgot to.

EAMON McGUINNESS

is from Dublin, Ireland. He holds
an MA in Creative Writing from University
College Dublin. His poetry has appeared in
*Poetry Ireland Review, Southword, Abridged, The
Honest Ulsterman, Crannóg, Skylight 47, Looking at
the Stars, Boyne Berries, The Bohemyth, Bare Hands
Poetry* and *Wordlegs*. In 2017, he was featured on
the Poetry Jukebox in Belfast and shortlisted for
the Strokestown International Poetry Prize.

THAT'S MY BODY

That's my body you saw floating,
mentioned on the nine o'clock news.
Paint-flecked, crow's feet, my body
with its ripped flaws, lumps, long nails,
bald-head birthmark, coast road curves,
sea-view eyes, unpainted house, abandoned car,
my body, bandwagoned, the one you see,
the one you can't. Anywhere dry take me,
I'll make it work, I'll work, I'll lie down,
I'll sleep, anywhere dry, anywhere.

That was my body,
squeezed into a tight-fitting drum.
In a past life I was suit-starched, pressed.
That's all of me, swollen and broken,
the way you can't tell these things
if the eyes are closed.
But I lived in space and for a time
something held me from leaving.

A body that lied to me,
newspapers in languages
I couldn't understand.
That's my body
in photo-of-the-year competitions,
in the puddle-push stroke
of a close-sea January,
clouds on top like ceilings.
But just to be in water,
that's what I thought,
just to be in water.

No one to bury me.
I learnt the word 'goodbye' in every language.
'Sorry' in Greek and Turkish.
I hid in the suburbs, in spare rooms,
avoided emails, late nights, friends, family, the papers.
Unlearnt words, erased thoughts,
I found new heroes, on stamps, at bus stops, in magazines.
That's my body, the one you're still carrying,
bulging, with the tag still on, documents lost,
nails grown back, tongue freshly painted,
my body, holding generations, forgotten.

No one said it was mine,
that I could keep it and use it as I wished,
no one told me to look after it,
that it was precious, unique and only for me.
My shoes aren't waterproof.
My t-shirt is plain white,
cheap but comfortable and pasted onto my skin like a tattoo.
I hear them above me, pulling, grabbing, lifting.
Their talk is of the weekend, one of them is smoking,
I can taste it. My eyes can't open to see.
I hear him say: 'Yes, you could put a suit on
this one, he's ready to go now.'

Yes, just wake him up,
put a suit on him
you could take that body anywhere.

REISS McGUINNESS

is a poet and photographer
living in Bath, UK. He has just completed
his MA in Creative Writing at Bath Spa and is
working on compiling poems around a project.
He currently works as a photographer, poetry
editor and in many trivial temp jobs.

THE SILENT TREATMENT

We sit at opposite ends of the table.
The lights are off. The curtains are open.

The moon is moving the shadow of the window frame
across the carpet, over the chair, the settee – you;

a cross-shaped shadow spanning hairline to chin,
crawling down your neck, your chest,

along the table and over me
before leaving us in darkness.

PAUL McMAHON

From Belfast, Paul McMahon's debut poetry chapbook, *Bourdon*, was published by Southword Editions in November, 2016. He was awarded The Keats-Shelley Poetry Prize by Carol Ann Duffy in 2015. Other poetry awards include 1ˢᵗ prize in The Ballymaloe International Poetry Prize, The Nottingham Open Poetry Prize, The Westport Poetry Prize and The Golden Pen Poetry Prize. Twice nominated for The Forward Prize, his poetry has appeared in journals such as *The Irish Times*, *The Threepenny Review*, *The Atlanta Review*, *Southword*, *The Salt Anthology of New Writing*, *The Montreal Poetry Prize Global Anthology*, *The Stinging Fly*, *Moth*, *Agenda*, *Ambit*, *Orbis*, and others.

THE PUPS IN THE BOGHOLE

I poured the milk into the cup
of hot black tea until the surface
clouded over and lightened,
with coils of steam,
like the genie of memory
rising out from the uncorked
bottle of the forgotten.

The turf-brown tea settled
at the brim of the cup,
as silent as the guilty bog-water
that brimmed the wide boghole
I had walked away from,
many years ago, when I was a child.

It was a deep boghole, a blind eye,
beside a bare oak tree whose branches,
like exposed nerve endings, signposted
its fatal spot in the middle
of the vast gouged-out turf-fields.

As I returned, that day,
to Uncle Frank's pub on the sea-road,
through the coconut scent
of the yellow whin bushes,
the palms of my hands
were still stinging, reddened,
branded by the weight and
the coarse fabric of the turf-sack

and all around was the echoing
liquid call of the curlew

83

marking out the hollow tent
of the sky – the amphitheatre
that had been listening all along
to the puppy-yelps muffled
in the turf-sack, and my footsteps
dragging them to the boghole.

The mute colosseum
of the firmament gasped
as the tossed sack
whirred through the air,
hit the bull's eye
of the boghole, bobbed,
seemed to float,
then slowly sank.

As I turned and fled
my footsteps were lighter
but the naivety of my bravery
weighed down
my outsized wellington boots
with a heavier tread – in my pocket

was the fifty pence piece,
the Judas-coin Uncle Frank
had given me to do the man's job
he didn't have time to do,
and overhead, the crowded
audience of the sky
darkened in disbelief.

*

As I sit here, years later,
and lift the teacup to my lips,

I realise I have been bringing
sacks to that boghole ever since –

the pups of what I cannot reveal
to anyone, pushing the visage
of their cave-art paws
out through the sacking,

and in my head I can still hear
Uncle frank's *well-greased till*
shoot open like a bullet
and hit home with a ring.

And I still see, beside the boghole,
on the wizened trunk of that burnt oak tree,

the eye of a twisted knot
staring out like the drowned.

– first appeared in *Eborakon*

CYNTHIA MILLER

is a Malaysian-American poet
and Brand Strategist. Her poems have
been published in *Primers Volume 2, The Emma
Press Anthology of Love, Butcher's Dog* and *Under
the Radar*, and shortlisted for the Bridport
Poetry Prize. She is also Co-Founder and
Co-Director of Verve, the Birmingham
Festival of Poetry and Spoken Word.

AUBADE WITH COURT RULING

Stand with me in the full fat American sunshine in all the places where we love each other: across state lines, courthouse steps, porch swings with seventeen fireflies for lamps, nothing forgotten or lost. Let me tell you about the orderly pursuit of happiness, summer undeterred, sucking stars on your shoulder, police vans swaying like sleep-warm bodies in the dark, the road always turning home. My beautiful boy, don't be afraid of loving. Are you getting all this down? There can be no question. There can be no doubt of liberty. Let me tell you who to love – no. Let me tell you how – yes: earth smelling of good mint, a skinny beanpole of a guy, the long lick of your back a furnace, sweet sweat pooling behind knees. The officer's expression like a door in the face and better a door than a fist, better a fist than your body bowing in the stand, good suit creasing, and better a body in a stand than in a tree. This is what I mean when I say unruly, you stubborn thing. Look at us, improper. Look at us, indecent. Look at us, incandescent and loving.

– first appeared in *Primers Volume 2*

In June 1967, the Supreme Court of the United States unanimously ruled in Loving v. Virginia that interracial marriage was constitutional.

AUDREY MOLLOY

was born in Dublin and grew up
in Blackwater, County Wexford. She practiced
optometry in Dublin before travelling to Syd-
ney, where she works as an optometrist and
medical writer. Her poetry has been widely
published, most recently in *Crannóg, Meanjin,
Australian Poetry Journal, Cordite, Headstuff, Ink,
Sweat & Tears* and *The Ofi Press*. In 2017 Molloy
received special commendation for the Patrick
Kavanagh Poetry Award. She was shortlisted for
the Noel Rowe Poetry Award 2017-18 and for the
Fool for Poetry International Chapbook Com-
petition 2017. She was also shortlisted for 2017
for the Bridport Prize, the Judith Wright Poetry
Prize for New and Emerging Poets and the Over
The Edge New Writer of the Year.

SYMPHONY OF SKIN

i. Tuning up

They are there if you listen.
On the train, in the laundromat –
the instruments, I mean;
bells, stirring in two-way stretch cotton,
(their owner slumped in the window seat,
his work boots tapping a secret rhythm);
timpani buttoned under a cashier's blouse,
a cello bound by polyester pinafore
in salmon pink. She thinks
the air is flecked with soap dust,
doesn't realise it's rosin from her bow.
Air flows through apertures
where, later, fingers will flutter,
strings blur under the rub of horsehair;
their discordant mewl barely heard
above the swish of the train,
the hum of machine,
louder in the darkness of tunnel
or the lull of rinse cycle, then soft again.
Tuning up, they're getting ready
for this evening's symphony of skin
to begin at precisely 10.15.

ii. Skin music

And you can never explain it in physical terms –
what happens between two people
on an ordinary bed, in an ordinary room.
Let me ask you, could you school the cuttlefish
in Ludwig's *Emperor* (second movement)

in terms of anvil, hammer and stirrup?
Paint the hues of daybreak for the mole?
There is only air, compressed and stretched.
There is always space between skins,
no matter how closely they press.
No touch, only the music of skin;
an oboe sings, a cello answers.
Locked within the strands of collagen,
atoms built of smaller blocks,
each one a capsule packed with strings,
each string a note that's yet to play.

iii. Reverberation

Afterwards, they lie curled,
two bass clefs facing this way, that.
They talk of anything, of childhood;
croak the lyrics to every Paul Simon song
they can recall; this, the highlight,
now the players have left the stage.
They will meet people
who promise them more than this,
more than you could write about this.
Sleep will come later, a raft
pushed out on a starred sea.
What oak bed? Which room?
There is nothing here
but phosphorescence
undulating along their border.
Only this tiny stage
drifting on the night swell,
a single baton on its floor.

– first appeared in *Meanjin*

CIAN MURPHY

was born and raised in Cork
and now lives between London and Bristol.
Murphy is Treasurer of the Bristol Poetry
Institute. He has published poems and
reviews in *Envoi*, *The Honest Ulsterman*,
Ink, Sweat & Tears, and
PN Review.

AT THE CLINIC

The winter trees have been laid bare.

A yellow digger reaches underneath
to shift earth from the bedrock.

Workers sink pylons and join slabs
of concrete with veins of steel.

Inside she does what she's told.

Breathe easy when they notch
her breastbone like Ogham.

Stay still now when the x-ray extends
on its accordion arm and thunks as

it finds its target.

Later, in the room next door,
nothing detects

the quicken of pulse
as the acetate slips
on the backlit table.

The digger shunts a rock aside.
The earth exhales. *Breathe easy*.

ALYCIA PIRMOHAMED

is a Canadian-born poet living in Scotland. She
is a PhD student at the University of Edinburgh,
where she is studying poetry by second-gener-
ation immigrant writers. She received an MFA
from the University of Oregon in 2014. Pir-
mohamed is the Creative Writing and Reviews
editor at *HARTS & Minds*, and she co-edits the
multilingual publication, *The Polyglot*. Her work
has recently appeared in *Prairie Schooner, Glass:
A Journal of Poetry, wildness, Grain Maga-
zine,* and *Vallum Magazine.*

ELEGY ON LOOP

Like taking the moon and salting it
      – gritty crystal,   bone body love,
all of the impulses

           I have asked my muscles to forget:
unfurling, seizing, concaving.

No one told me loss was like *this*.
      This dark grey bar rising like an ugly statistic.

This wild bitterness, unripe blackberry, mouthful
of dirt.

         This shadow – midnight crow with a
crushed spine, wingless.

Like taking the moon and slicing it   evenly.
      One-half stone, one-half heartache,

and in its entirety, an elegy playing on loop.
      This is deletion.

I guess this is the kind of erasure I always feared.
      The kind of opaque nothingness that asks me to
open my fist

      – only to let go.

This world constantly gives into its laws.   Mathematics.
      The equation that marks me

with an x. Balance. You on the other side.

– first appeared in *Grain*

KERRY PRIEST

grew up in Sheffield and studied
Anthropology and Linguistics at Edinburgh
University. She has lectured in English and
Cultural Studies at Eichstaett and Humboldt
Universities in Germany, as well as DJing for
many years at some of Europe's biggest clubs and
festivals. She presents a show on Soundart Radio
102.5 FM which combines poetry with experi-
mental improvised electronic music. Kerry has
been published in *The Broadsheet* and shortlisted
for the Bridport and Bradford on Avon prizes.

THE UNINTENTIONAL SIDE-BENEFITS
OF A SLOW AND PREMATURE DEATH

You're a slice of cake
wrapped in greaseproof paper
tied with string in a neat bow
symmetrical and just so.

You're a hand-drawn map
in copper plate you show
Honeysuckle Cottage,
Rufford Abbey, the river.

You're immaculate sheets
airing on sunny lines
pressed and stacked in
scented drawers.

You'll never be a shaking hand
popping pegs in the biscuit tin
as your favourite coasters
melt in the toaster

never be found
down the shops in your nightie
frozen-eyed, lamb-lost,
calling my name in the rain.

MICHAEL RAY

is a poet and glass artist living in
West Cork, Ireland. His poems have
appeared in a number of Irish and international
journals, including *The Moth, The Irish Independent,
The Shop, Cyphers, The Penny Dreadful, One,
Southword, The Stinging Fly, Ambit* and *Magma*.
In 2012 he was a winner in the Fish International
poetry competition. In 2013 he was shortlisted for
the Hennessey award. In 2016, he won the Poetry
Ireland Café poetry competition. His visual art
has been collected by the Irish Craft and
Design Council, the Department for
Foreign Affairs and the National
Museum of Ireland.

ZEST

Take one from the bowl.
Hold it in your palm, navel up, as if
still growing; as though it were the world.
Let in the nail of your thumb.
Take care; the rind must come off in one.
Even blind, you can circumnavigate
its umbilicus, peel away ice fields,
tundra, blue-eyed iris grass and krill.

The orange flesh will turn, its pith
orbiting as fingers strip forests
holding undiscovered rain,
Appalachian fens, snowshoe hares.
There goes a shining sunrise
ocean, great clouds of silver fish.
Birds screech as they wheel
around a spiralling of rind.

Don't stop; there's more to pare.
Red deer; blue oyster mushrooms
letting go their spores.
Now open out the fleshy sphere,
its unexploded sacs of seed.
The empty rind will wind back up,
appear intact. To implode will take
some time. By then you will be gone.

– first appeared in *A Change of Climate*

SHAUNA ROBERTSON

was born in the north-east of
England and now lives in the south-west.
She has two poetry pamphlets, *Blueprints for a
Minefield* (Fair Acre Press, 2016) and *Love Bites*
(Dancing Girl Press, 2018). Her poems appear in
a wide range of journals and anthologies
and some have been set to music, performed
by actors, displayed on buses, hung on a pub
wall and turned into comic art. Shauna also
writes for children. Her artwork has featured
in publications and exhibitions.

GINGER

I'll never forget, says Uncle Malc,
that time when Ginger Rogers tripped on the two-step
and tumbled head first from Hollywood to Hartlepool.

We all rushed down to the shore
and took turns nudging the washed-up body
with our loafers and creepers.
To check for signs of life, we said,
though really, each of us hoped
to make an impression.

Dreamed of how, later,
over a steaming Bovril she'd ask,
Whose were those light-as-a-feather tootsies,
the tippy-toes in white winkle-pickers?
Now those belong to a hoofer and a half!
Then she'd call Fred and tell him
she'd found her 'Top Hat' and wasn't coming back.

We waited and waited.
Then I guess we moved on.
In the end it was young Tyrone next door
who finally made it to L.A.,
but by then poor Ginger was picked clean by seagulls
and the old musicals had pretty much had their day.

– first appeared in *Under the Radar*

LENNI SANDERS

is a writer and performer based in
Manchester. She makes interactive
performances with Curious Things and
poetry cabaret with Dead Lads. Her writing has
appeared in print and online magazines includ-
ing *The Tangerine, Butcher's Dog,* and *The Real
Story,* and is forthcoming in the *Emma Press
Anthology of Love.*

NYE

Overnight I found I'd switched places with my shadow,
dressed it in my buttonless overcoat and stained knickers, and now
I cannot move without shame. Winter and, I am trying.

    The new year comes
like a huge dog out of the bushes
like a tooth from a mouth
like a barrel over a waterfall
like me, inside a barrel, over a waterfall

This year I feel like it will be important somehow to keep an electric shock
shuttling around inside ourselves: it will be the time to keep our fingers
in the plug sockets

  and this is the year, also, to sleep attentively
to coax dreams in. Sleep close to fish-tanks, windows, faces:
anything you can see at once through and into. Use your discretion
I guess.

The eggshell of the year breaks as the beak comes through.
In a room so full I can't really move
I kiss my friend on the cheek and half an hour later
I'm throwing up and I'm sobbing
                and I'm sobbing and

I am making resolutions
  although they are only
a kind of jigsaw puzzle you arrange and put in order
then, with satisfaction, cram back in the box and into the cupboard

I will make a fool of myself again. Unabashed,
I will lose my speechlessness. I will scrape the fear off me
with the back of a spoon the same way you peel ginger.

– first appeared in *The Tangerine*

BREDA SPAIGHT

was born in Co. Limerick,
Ireland, 1957. She was among the poets
accepted to the Poetry Ireland Introductions
Series 2017, and the Introductions Readings
at the Cork International
Poetry Festival 2018.

MY MOTHER'S WILL

after Polly Clark

To the Maguires – the neighbours: my high hedge,
gleaming windows & locked gate.
To my daughter: the clock with the missing minute hand.
To my eldest son: my apron strings.
To my middle son: my maroon & white silk scarf.
To my youngest son: the five candles from his birthday cake.
To my husband: our daughter.
To my sister: my stationery and pens, sewing machine,
good coat, knitting needles & Royal Doulton tea set.
To my daughter in addition: my children, poultry, geraniums
& wedding ring.
To the Maguires in addition: the tablecloth
that blew from their clothesline, & their children's football.

ALEXANDRA STRNAD

read English at the University of Cambridge, and graduated with a Master's in Creative Writing, with Distinction, from the University of Oxford. She was the 2014 Winner of the Jane Martin Poetry Prize and a 2016 Winner of the Oxford University Parallel Universe Poetry Competition. A dual Czech-British national, she lived in Prague for several years. Her first pamphlet *H is for Hadeda* was published by Poetry Salzburg in 2017. She is Poet-in-Residence at Carfax Education.

THE EYEMOUTH TAPESTRY

1

Men fell like apples, making no dent
in the harbour's soil. One thousand
stitches to raise each face, and storm
clouds threaded in French wool.

Two hands remain on deck, oiled
hats pulled low, one with a mouth
broke open to the Hundertwasser
blue: the mad, slabber-white foam.

2

Now the women weave a roundel
of ocean fruit, for lives defined
by crab, flounder, cod; for boys
raised in peat-smoke, vennels

of youth; for all that knew peril
and shrugged it off. Quiet thimbles
dress the dead as mothers who tie
the boot-laces of a child – rusted

eyelets looped with kelp and coral
weed. Their hair turns the colour
of October, tides peel a bride's
cheek to bone, sands sink her feet.

3

Only petit point and Gobelin stitch
left to flesh the years, scratch the past,
make it heal. A pentaptych is born –
a palette of kaleidoscope dyes,

here, the wheelhouse meets the sun
in shafts of gold, umber, sable,
sea swells are subdued by fingertips,
and needles bring the calm.

– first appeared in *Ambit* and the *Aesthetica Creative Writing Annual 2017*

The Eyemouth disaster occurred on the 14th October 1881. One hundred and eighty-nine men from Eyemouth and neighbouring fishing towns lost their lives. This event is commemorated in the 'Eyemouth Tapestry'.

SARAH STUTT

is studying for a PhD in Creative
Writing at the University of Hull. She has
had poems published in *Poetry Salzburg Review*,
The North, *The Yellow Nib*, and *Iota*. Her first
poetry pamphlet, *Winter Born*, was published by
Poetry Salzburg Press in 2017.

LETATLIN *(BUILT BETWEEN 1929 AND 1931)*

Vladimir Tatlin came up with the name by combining
the Russian word 'letat', meaning 'to fly', and his last name.

A fly's abdomen teased apart
with tweezers, the musculature
of a pigeon, its glossy purple heart
in his palm, the modest theatre
of each grey wing, unfolding
in his thick, simple fingers.

Vladimir's fragile flying machine
made from ashwood and hubris,
held together with whalebone.
We shall fly higher than Icarus
in this hand-crafted ribcage where
the body lies flat, suspended in air.

He pedals his new, insectoid bird
across the field towards the sun
in his overalls, a dress rehearsal
for flight, a hopeful revolution.
Silk-skinned wings tremble, resist
the lure of any skyward drift.

He tinkers for two more years,
adjusts and tweaks his limitless art
until the New Order changes gear,
back-tracks on its fresh start.
Now it hangs from a false ceiling
and all these hearts are darkening.

ROSAMUND TAYLOR

is from Dublin. In 2017, she won
the inaugural Mairtín Crawford Award at
the Belfast Book Festival. She has been nomi-
nated for a Pushcart Prize (2015) and a Forward
Prize (2017) by *Crannóg Magazine*. She has twice
been short-listed for the Montreal International
Poetry Prize, and her work has most recently
appeared in *Magma* and *Agenda*.

DEATH'S-HEAD HAWKMOTH

It's frightening to be so ill.
I take the heat of my body outside, I lie
limp on dew-wet grass. I feel myself
shake, keep shaking.
The death's-head a thought, then a flicker.

~

In Arizona, hummingbirds
come to garden feeders filled
with nectar instead of seed. Birds
are vivid as flowers, beaks flash
like coins. In Dublin, after dark,
I see a death's-head hawkmoth,
wings jagged as torn paper.

~

The hawkmoth shadowing the lilac leaves.
Do everything you want to do. Do it at once.

~

Your legs don't seem enough to hold you –
perhaps you never walk, perhaps like a swift
you are always on the wing.
I could crush you in my hands.

~

The princess jabs her finger on a spindle:
like the moment before

111

I touch the moth's wings, the bands
of yellow and of black –

the silence after.

~

Granite stairs, uneven, overgrown.
Each step cast in orange shadow
by the street-light. The smell of curry,
of drains, and, low, the honeysuckle.
The hawkmoth, a sudden blur,
a dusty god. I am alone.

~

Crumbling in the museum display,
the death's-head hawkmoth, wings open like a question.

JONATHAN TOTMAN

was born in Sussex in 1987.
He studied psychology and philosophy
before going on to train as a clinical
psychologist. His poems have appeared
in magazines including *Brittle Star*, *Envoi*, *The
Frogmore Papers*, *The Interpreter's House*, *Lighthouse*
and *Orbis*. His debut pamphlet, *Explosives Licence*,
was a winner in the 2018 iOTA Shot Pamphlet
Competition. Jonathan was the Fenland Poet
Laureate for 2015 and co-founded *The Fenland
Reed*, a magazine for new writing.

EXPLOSIVES LICENCE

Is there anything you want to ask me
before we go in? I laugh
as you unlock the three locks

to the shed, my ten-year-old hands
sliding to coat pockets
for matches I know aren't there.

Inside, your industrial flashlight
flits over cardboard boxes:
Kimbolton Fireworks.

Racks of mortar tubes,
gaffer tape, hard hats,
brown paper-wrapped shells.

I stand still as you rifle.
Sandstorm, Star Mine.
Twist of quick-fuse at my feet.

I've seen you on show night:
nervy, quiet, ducking under
yellow tape in a high-vis jacket,

fading to a figure with a spark.
Later, you show me how to fuse up
rockets at the dining room table,

head bent over a soldering iron.
Peony, Tiger Willow,
Hummingbird, Roman Candle.

— first appeared in *Brittle Star*

SARAH WALLIS

was born in London,
in 1974 and now works as a poet
and playwright in Leeds. Recent publications
include the *Yorkshire Poetry Anthology* from
Valley Press and *Watermarks; for Lido Lovers
and Wild Swimmers* by the Frogmore Press.
Theatrical residencies include West
Yorkshire Playhouse and Harrogate
Theatre, supporting her works
The Rain King and *Laridae*.

THE WORLD STANDS STILL TO WEEP

Zero point zero zero two five grams
is the weight of a tear. Think of the person

whose job it is to know it,
to pursue that knowledge in a white coat

not given to just anyone, to note the rare
specimens in urgent copperplate, clear

and perfectly formed as snowflakes make lone
journeys of sorrow, the sink of it, the simple

warp and weft, a streaking pearl
of headlamp, a lone motorcyclist at dawn

and heartbreak crawling
across the clean sheet of a cheek.

Imagine the interview for such a post,
the seeking out of the sort most sensitive

for this work that should be the provenance
of the tooth-fairy's cousins, flickering light

barely disturbing a flutter of wings, as they reach
with a feather for this most precious of things,

carrying a pair of tiny gold scales
for the measuring out and testing the weight

of fragile beauty, the salt content
of nature's mirror-ball to be panned for

and collected, like rubies or spice.

– first appeared in *Magic Oxygen Anthology*

JACK WARREN

is originally from the southwest of
England. His work has appeared in *Anomaly
Literary Journal* as well as *Allegro Poetry* and he
won first prize at the Prague International
Micro-Festival in 2017. He has lived in Greece
and the Czech Republic, and is currently study-
ing for an MA at the University of York.

STILL LIFE WITH PLASTIC CARRIER BAG

It could be hazel or it could be ash
but who knows the names of trees anymore?
I used to see my breath in winter air
as proof of an inner life – diaphragm
lungs, sutured into a body that turned
corners; smiled at strangers in shopping centres.
Now I cling to the world like the carrier
entangled in the branches of this tree,
hollow and corrupting and complicit.
Too ungrateful to look up from my phone,
too stupid and lazy to call my mum
and tell her everything will be okay.
Do you remember the iridescent
blue of that damselfly as it laid eggs
in the watercourse near the Stockhill Wood?
How unwieldy, liquid and alien
it looked, hovering its thorax over
the forest debris of leaf mould, beech seeds?
I must find a way to be that awestruck
again. Rapt, gazing at something outside
myself. Gawping at the temerity
of the world, to be so bravely normal.

SUSAN WATSON

grew up in Eastwood, Nottinghamshire
(the birthplace of D.H. Lawrence). Her poems
have appeared in *The Rialto*, *Brittle Star*, *The
Frogmore Papers* and in the anthologies *A Room
to Live In* (Salt Publishing) and *Herrings*
(Blue Door Press). She is completing a
PhD in Creative Writing at
Goldsmiths, University
of London.

PAUL AND CLARA WALK BESIDE THE TRENT

The mind can be too busy, struggling to forge significance,
making this mean that exact thing, hammering it down.
No detail is left alone to dart quickly along like a gleam of light on water,
to drift in the atmosphere like the scent of wild thyme on the wind.
There are real rivers that flow unnaturally fast and silent,
a film speeded up, but suppose an inflamed young man
walks out with a married woman, gets stuck in red mud.
The river is swirling from heavy rain. There is a footprint
left by a man's nailed boot. This can be read
as a reminder of the woman's discarded husband.
His possible vengeance. Her sexual experience.
I know that red mud. I know that it gathers under the instep,
upsetting the balance, builds itself into a wedge right under the heel,
soaks the shoe through.

This river moves like a subtle and complex animal.
We don't quite say a snake. There are currents like trailing hair.
And the couple appear to be trapped with no way forward.
Then the footprint. A tentative path can be trodden by one pair of feet.
An escape, or a possible way. A reminder
that this particular couple were never alone in the world.
I have walked like that on my own,
catching at twigs and brambles and I know
that each tread is important and must be tested
before the ground can be trusted to bear the weight.
Each handhold is vital, each thorn is important, each streak of damp green.
Red mud goes everywhere.

He must have known this. It was a real place.

– first appeared in *The Rialto*

CHRISTIAN WETHERED

was selected for the 2017 Poetry
Ireland Introductions Series. He was third-
placed in the 2017 Cafe Writers Poetry Competi-
tion, and has been published in *The Moth,
Brittle Star* and *The Caterpillar*. He was also
featured in the anthology *In the Cinnamon
Corner* (Cinnamon Press).

LETHE

after Baudelaire

I like to lick its hole with my tongue,
listen to it melting, widen, soften.

When I kiss it will follow,
easing to muscle like a lip —

it lets you in; and once in, the space
is warm, dark — the inside of a

mountain, invisible but such tenderness
there to stretch. It sucks you back

when you give, lets you in. Try the
whole hand if you like, the smell is

tipped with sugary sweat, something
luxurious and soapy. The inside is

an aroma you've never tried;
stale, yes, dark and ripe.

MARIAH WHELAN

was born in Oxford in 1986.
She studied English at Queen's University
Belfast, has an MSt in Creative Writing from
the University of Oxford and is currently based
in the Centre for New Writing at The Univer-
sity of Manchester, where she writes poems and
researches trauma and memory in Irish fiction.
Mariah's poetry has been shortlisted for the
Bridport Prize and the Melita Hume Prize and
won the A.M. Heath Prize, and she is current-
ly Poet-in-Residence of the Post-War Seminar
Series at the University of Oxford.

HEFTED

One by one the black-faced ewes
file through the gate. Up and out of the field

over the burned heather to lamb
where their mothers lambed them.

I try to pull a map around the stories:
I know here is where my father was happiest –

if I sit on this rock and let the same cold
enter my body can I say I'm part of it?

Plates of ice across the mud crack under weight,
catch light like the light is something

good enough to frame and hang
in a hall where guests first enter.

His maps were always like that –
half an advertisement of character,

half a mirror to hold the face that looked
square in its white mount.

On and on, the hundred or so ewes file through
hefted to the particular slope that bore them.

Muscle memory, DNA, where do their bodies hold
the bone-hunger that leads them back,

precise as a compass point finding its way
through layers of tracing paper and folded map

to hold its beam-arm straight –
making the distance between them measurable.

JAMES A. H. WHITE

was born in Surrey, England. A first-generation
Japanese-British immigrant, and former resident
of New Zealand, he received his MFA in Cre-
ative Writing at Florida Atlantic University as
a Lawrence A. Sanders poet fellow. Author of
the chapbook *hiku [pull]* (Porkbelly Press, 2016),
James is the winner of an AWP Intro Journals
Project award and five-time Pushcart Prize
nominee with writing published in *Black Warrior
Review*, *Cha: An Asian Literary Journal*, *Colorado
Review*, *Quarterly West*, and *Washington Square
Review*, among others.

ASTROBIOLOGY

suggests there's a whole lot more out there
than other fish in other seas.

I tell Florida Prisoner X
while Prisoner Y shoots hoops
Mars has never been closer,

so he paints five white men
against a wash of red
& asks if I know what he did.

*Yes – you painted five men
who aren't you.*

Prisoner Y shouts from across the gymnasium,
*You're not talking about the same thing, man.
You never are.*

In my painting: a man with his face hidden
beneath a conical hat throws a fishing net
where he last saw water.

Above him: a blue koi & gold koi circle
each other, head to tail. Their moon: somehow
I say, a never-ending splash.

Its orbit, kept to myself: everything
I remembered this morning while walking
down the driveway to the mailbox
about a former dance professor who said
a good dancer knows their limits
so they can be broken, & felt

each girl's coccyx to explain
whether or not they'll have a painful childbirth.

The impossible cause
of what I both hope & fear:
I tell Prisoner X about the hole
behind the man – a cave where he keeps
a stool, a blanket, & a daughter
he told is too young to understand.

In the same bright pond

of memory, I leave the compound
waist-deep in unknowing.

Space don't look like that, man,
he'd said, returning to his desk
while the basketball rolled
casually toward a blocked door.

You don't know what I've painted,
I'd responded, adding more blue
to the koi I've named after no one he knows.

Man, I already know you drawn
some fucked up shit, man.
This is reality in here. You got blue
on your brush. There ain't no
blue for miles in here.

127

Answer: it's quieter up there, Houston.

Answer: you could just give the man the water he needs.

Answer: how long have they been up there, in Earth
years?

Well, what do you think
the edge of space looks like, Y?

Answer: he loses either way.

Answer: there's either nothing he wants
                or everything he's lost.

Question for the warden
after the fifth class: did you know
koi fish have teeth? Prisoner X told me
they're in the back of their throat.

It's just, what a place to keep the important things –

It's just, the man I think I am or deserve
doing what he can to survive –

It's just, he used to catch so much there.

PATRICK WRIGHT

was born in 1979. He completed
a PhD in English at the University of Man-
chester in 2007, supervised by Professor Terry
Eagleton. He graduated, more recently, with an
MA (Distinction) from the same university in
Creative Writing, and is now working towards
a second PhD at the Open University, focusing
on ekphrastic poems in response to modernist
painting. He also teaches Arts and Humanities
modules, including Creative Writing. His poetry
pamphlet, *Nullaby*, was published by Eyewear in
2017. His poems have appeared in several maga-
zines and anthologies, and he has been shortlist-
ed for the Bridport Prize.

THE END

With the close of a hospice door, clunk of a saloon, tyres
on gravel: an ending if ever there was one. Let us slalom
round statues of Mary, grottos in grounds, funerary fetishes.

Let it end with handed-over possessions, towels, slippers,
photo off the wall (she never saw), smell of softened linens,
folded neatly with inventory, for no one especially.

Ask for no heroes, villains, nick-of-time pliers on wires,
no H-bomb to defuse on the horizon. Ask for nothing
as the sun pops, extinguishes. Let it end as a balloon.

Let the chauffeur pull unsmilingly through the driveway.
Let the leaves fall sometimeish in September.
Let unhappy accidents happen on dual carriageways.

See father as a mannequin, us *both* as mannequins, feel
the numbness of thumbs on a gear lever, steering wheel
turn, sink in a blue lagoon, birds scatter from traffic islands.

Let doctors be anything but miracle workers. Sack Christ,
alienists. Insist the priest toddle off with his rosary beads,
chuck out his wooden crosses, fuck off to the hypermarket.

Pray only clouds on roads chaperone us. Stay on auto-pilot.
Read of St Bede's swiftness of sparrow down a dining hall.
Let's go art house, kino lounge a while:

130

Let bus stops hang unseasonal icicles, Belisha beacons
be lollipops if they want, the forget-me-nots freeze,
apocalyptic winter, denouement leave all threads a tangle.

Then *fin*, fade to dark. Stars drip to stalactites.

– first appeared in *Agenda*

MAGGIE SMITH

is the author of *Good Bones* (Tupelo
Press, 2017); *The Well Speaks of Its Own Poison*
(2015), winner of the Dorset Prize; *Lamp of the Body*
(Red Hen Press, 2005), winner of the Benjamin
Saltman Award; and three prizewinning chapbooks.
Her poems have appeared in the *New York Times*,
the *Paris Review*, the *Best American Poetry*, the *Kenyon
Review*, *AGNI*, *Ploughshares*, and elsewhere. Smith
is the recipient of fellowships from the National
Endowment for the Arts, the Ohio Arts Council, and
the Sustainable Arts Foundation. In 2016 her poem
'Good Bones' went viral internationally and was
called the 'Official Poem of 2016' by Public Radio
International.

TODD SWIFT

is the Montreal-born, British
founder-director of Eyewear Publishing,
based in London and now in its 7th year. His own
poems are Selected by Salmon in Ireland and Marick
in the USA. He has edited or co-edited over a dozen
anthologies since 1988, including *The Poet's Quest
For God*. His latest pamphlet is *Madness & Love In Maida
Vale* (2016). His PhD is from the UEA, on style in mid-
century British poets, notably Tiller and Prince. His
essays on poetry have recently appeared in academic
publications from Palgrave and the University of
Liverpool, as well as in *Poetry* magazine and *Poetry
London*. He was included in *The Oxford Companion
to Modern Poetry in English*. He is the 2017/18
Writer-in-residence for Pembroke College,
Cambridge University.

EYEWEAR PUBLISHING